Recipe for Stress-free Homework

PRAISE of the Book

"We don't always get to choose what happens in this life, but we can choose to grow in compassion and wisdom as a result. This book offers valuable, practical methods for doing so."

—Dr. Roopinder Dogra
MBBS, DNB (Obstetrics & Gynaecology) and Author of "Prisms of Life"
(Currently actively practicing in Kuwait)

"Having just read this book I wanted to thank you for it. It's fascinating and inspirational — every parent should read it."

—Deepak Sharma
Author of 'Move Mountain'

"This is a lovely book, a moving account of a difficult passage, full of heart and wisdom."

— Dr. A.K. saini
(Professor), IPU, Delhi
Ph.D., M.Phill. (Physics), M.Sc., MCA, MBA, FIETE, MAIMA

This book is selected by National Book Trust(NBT), Government of India at:

- **South Africa Book Fair, 2012**
- **China International Book Fair, 2013**

RECIPE FOR STRESS-FREE HOMEWORK

Learn how to make Homework Honey for your Kids

Worldwide Published by
Pendown Press

PENDOWN PRESS

An ISO 9001 & ISO 14001 Certified Co.,

Regd. Office: 2525/193, 1st Floor, Onkar Nagar-A,
Tri Nagar, Delhi-110035

Ph.: 09350849407, 09312235086

E-mail: info@pendownpress.com

Branch Office: 1A/2A, 20, Hari Sadan, Ansari Road,
Daryaganj, New Delhi-110002

Ph.: 011-45794768

Website: PendownPress.com

First Edition: 2019

Price: ₹259/-

ISBN: 978-93-81970-04-1

Layout and Cover Designed by Pendown Graphics Team

Printed and Bound in India by Thomson Press India Ltd.

Contents

Few Words

Homework can be an important tool to help children review and practice the skills taught in school and improve their learning. In addition, homework can help enhance children's personal growth by teaching them responsibility, independent work habits, organization and time management. However, when problems arise, homework can be quite disruptive to family life by creating parent-child conflict and interfering with other important family priorities, such as recreation and social activities.

One of the more common homework problems reported by parents is poor motivation, particularly in families with children with learning or attention deficit disorders. Children who are described as motivated to do homework do it by themselves, begin and complete it on time, actively participate in checking it, respond well when told to correct it, pay attention during it, and stick with it even when it gets difficult. When children face problems with any of these areas of homework, they are frequently described as being "unmotivated".

Parents' beliefs and practices put heavy influences on children's success. Therefore, try and help your child see homework as an opportunity, not a threat. Tell your child very often that you think homework is very important. Get involved in homework postponing your own works. Never use homework as a punishment and never kids exempt their homework as a reward.

Make your kids believe that their homework cannot wait for a day, but all other works can. Educate them on the importance of homework and how completing homework everyday will help them learn better and secure impressive marks in the class.

- Anita Verma

Acknowledgements

This edition of Recipe for Stress-free Homework has been possible with the contributions of many people. I would like to acknowledge and specially thank my husband Dinesh Verma for his expert guidance and too much encouragement. A special thanks to him for his valuable insights, critique, and constant support throughout the development of this book.

I would like to put in my appreciation and acknowledgement for my family members, relatives, friends and Team of Pendown Press and PendownPress.com.

I am especially grateful to the cause of concern of parents towards their children in every walk of life.

– Anita Verma

1 INTRODUCTION

"The real property that a parent can transmit to all equally is his or her character and educational facilities."
~ *Mahatma Gandhi*

Homework has been a part of students' lives since the beginning of formal schooling in India. However, the practice has sometimes been accepted and sometimes rejected, both by educators and parents. However, the importance of homework can never be undermined. The very fact that homework means reinforcement and generates constructive learning is something that needs to be understood. This has happened because homework can have both positive and negative effects on children's learning and attitudes towards school.

The Changing Phases

In the early times, the mind was viewed as a muscle that could be strengthened through mental exercise. Since exercise could be done at home, homework was viewed favorably. After that, schools began shifting their emphasis from memorization to problem solving. Since early 90s, when technological advancements (computer etc.) started influencing almost every sector, especially education Indians worried that education lacked rigor and left children unprepared for the new technologies, such as computers. Homework, it was believed, could speed up learning.

In today's modern times, educators and parents feel that homework is crowding out social experience, outdoor recreation and creative activities. In last two decades, homework again came back into favor as it came to be viewed as one way to stem a rising tide of mediocrity in Indian education. The push for more homework continued into the 1990s, fueled by rising academic standards.

Today there is a huge pressure on children for completion of projects and homework. It thus becomes imperative to make homework stress free. It becomes very important to make homework stress free and a learning experience!!

To Do or Not To Do Homework?

Homework–as long as there has been formal schooling there has been homework. Reactions to homework vary from a welcome challenge to stress overload for all involved: students, parents, and teachers. But like it or not, homework is here to stay. For those of you who associate the start of school with the potential for homework meltdowns, we offer some answers and helpful tips, suggestions, guidelines, and interventions on how to make the homework struggle a more stress-free and productive experience.

Research also indicates that homework is an excellent means of reinforcing and consolidating the information and skills your child learns at school. Second, homework has many potential benefits; it helps develop study skills, time management skills, independence and, most importantly, responsibility.

Homework can have many benefits for young children. It can improve remembering and understanding of schoolwork. Homework can help students to develop study skills that will be of value even after they leave school. It can teach them that learning takes place anywhere, not just in the classroom. Homework can benefit children in more general ways as well. It can foster positive character traits such as independence and responsibility. Homework can teach children how to manage time.

Homework, if not properly assigned and monitored, can also have negative effects on children. Educators and parents worry that students will grow bored if they are required to spend too much time on schoolwork. Homework can prevent children from taking part in leisure-time and community activities that also teach important life skills. Homework can lead to undesirable character traits if it promotes cheating, either through the copying of assignments or help with homework that goes beyond tutoring.

The issue for educators and parents is not which list of effects, the positive or negative is correct. To a degree, both the effects are true. It is the job of parents and educators to maximize the benefit of homework and minimize the time to get it completed. There are many ways that students drift into academic trouble: problems with homework are a common component of declining performance. Homework problems can quickly snowball into serious academic difficulties that may lead to undesirable consequences. It is important that a family find a plan that works for them and is effective. Whatever the plan and however you decide to implement it, the homework plan begins with you.

Is It Enough Homework?

The most critical question about homework is "How much homework should students do?" Experts agree that the amount of homework should depend on the age and skills of the student. Many national groups of teachers and parents suggest that homework for children in kindergarten through second grade is most effective when it does not exceed 10-20 minutes each day. In third through sixth grade, children can benefit from 30-60 minutes of homework per day. Junior high and high school students can benefit from more time on homework.

Reading at home is especially important for young children. High-interest reading assignments might push the time on homework a bit beyond the minutes suggested above.

These recommendations are consistent with the conclusions reached by many studies on the effectiveness of homework. For young children, research shows that shorter and more frequent assignments may be more effective than longer but fewer assignments. This is because young children have short spans of attention and need to feel they have successfully completed a task.

Types of Homework

Homework assignments typically have one or more purposes. The most common purpose is to have students practice material already presented in class:

- **Practice** homework is meant to reinforce learning and help the student in mastering specific skills.
- **Preparation** homework introduces material that will be presented in future lessons. These assignments aim to help students learn new material better when it is covered in class.

- **Extension** homework asks students to apply skills they already have to new situations.
- **Integration** homework requires the student to apply many different skills to a single task, such as book reports, science projects or creative writing.

In particular, math homework is regarded to be more important in the middle to high school grades in comparison with the elementary grades. It starts to become important in the fourth grade and is increasingly important in the upper grades.

How Parents Can Help with Homework?

Research also shows that parent involvement can have either a positive or negative impact on the value of homework. Parental involvement can be used to speed up a child's learning. Homework can involve parents in the school process. It can enhance parents' appreciation of education. It can give them an opportunity to express positive attitudes about the value of success in school.

But parental involvement may also interfere with learning. For example, parents can confuse children if the teaching techniques they use differ from those used in the classroom. Parent involvement in homework can turn into parents' interference if parents complete tasks that the child is capable of completing alone.

When mothers and fathers get involved with their children's homework, communication between the school and family tend to improve. It can clarify for parents what is expected of students. It can give parents a firsthand idea of what students are learning and how well their child is doing in school.

Researches show that if a child is having difficulty with homework, parents should become involved by paying close attention. They should expect more requests from teachers for their help. If a child is doing well in school, parents should consider shifting their efforts to providing support for their child's own choices about how to do homework. Parents should avoid interfering in the independent completion of assignments.

As this brief introduction suggests, homework can be an effective way for students to improve their learning and for parents to communicate their appreciation of schooling. Because a great many things influence the impact of homework achievement, expectations for homework's effects, especially in the earlier grades, must be realistic.

Homework policies and practices should give teachers and parents the flexibility to take into accounts the unique needs and circumstances of their students. That way, they can maximize the positive effects of homework and minimize the negative ones.

A Few Tips for Parents

- **Space:** Provide a quiet, well-lit place to complete homework. Make sure that all materials are available and avoid having the mobile or television to minimize distractions. Keep interruptions by siblings and friends relatives to a minimum as well.

- **Schedule:** Make studying, homework included, a daily habit. Don't ask your child if he has homework each night – assume that he always has homework or tasks to do. Establish a set time for homework and/or studying.

  It is not a good idea to do homework till bedtime or to leave long or involved projects for the last minute.

- **Model:** Model organizational techniques, work habits, and consider doing "adult homework" while your child completes his/her homework.

- **Attitude:** Show your child you think homework is important. The attitude you express about school and homework will be the attitude of your child. Set clear expectations.

- **Support:** Check homework and be available for assistance. When your child asks for help, provide guidance, NOT answers.

- **Involvement:** Take an active interest in your child's schooling. Be in contact with your child's teacher and do not wait until grades come out to discover there is a problem. Take your child's difficulties seriously; help devise a plan to assist him with difficulties at school.
- **Praise:** Praise your child for good effort, as well as good performance, as these will help him build self-esteem; maintain a portfolio of "best pieces" of work from school.

Specific Strategies for Assisting with Homework

- Use checklists and/or assignment books to help with organization of homework assignments. Set up file folders for each subject area to track papers or long-term assignments. Use a plastic bin or pencil box to store study materials. It is portable and accessible.
- Designate a study space and time. Use visuals such as clocks. It may be beneficial to use timers to signal when to start, when to stop, how much time is left, and when to take breaks. Use a calendar to break big projects into manageable chunks.
- Homework Contracts are useful and rewards, motivators, and/or incentives can be incorporated according to the likes of your child.

- Make a game out of homework completion – "place bets" or try to "beat the clock" based on how long it usually takes to finish assignments. A sample reinforcement system follows for completing work on time or ahead of schedule.
- You can develop a customized game spinner by using cardboard and brads, or you may purchase blank spinners from educational supply stores. Fill in each section of the spinner with a reward. Use tape so that you can occasionally change the rewards. Be sure to vary the prizes on the spinner so that some are more desirable. You may also want to have a space marked "no-win."
- Establish criteria with your child for completing homework assignments appropriately or finishing all homework tasks for the evening. When your child meets the criteria (*i.e.*, completes the task), allow him to use the spinner and earn the reward indicated. Be sure to use an appropriate positive statement such as, "Great job tonight!"
- To stop dependence on the spinner, gradually change the rewards to verbal praise and encouragement for homework completion.

xxx

Always kiss your children goodnight, even if they're already asleep.
~H. Jackson Brown, Jr.

2 HOMEWORK: A CONCERN FOR THE WHOLE FAMILY

"Let us Sacrifice our Today so that our
Children can have Better Tomorrow."
~ *APJ Abdul Kalam*

Homework is an opportunity for children to learn and for families to be involved in their children's education. However, helping children with homework isn't always easy. At parent-teacher meetings and in conferences with parents, teachers often hear questions such as:

- How can I get Sanjeev to do his homework? Every night it's a struggle to get him to turn off the TV and do his homework.
- Why isn't Mishti getting more homework?
- Why is Shefali getting so much homework?
- When is Mehar supposed to do homework? She takes dance classes, sings in her school assembly, plays basketball and helps with family chores. There's hardly any time left to study.
- How can I help Rohan with his math homework when I don't understand it?
- Do homework assignments really help my child learn?

This book helps answer these and other questions that parents, family members and others who care for children in elementary and middle school, often ask about homework. The book also includes practical ideas for helping children to complete homework assignments successfully.

×××

There is no job more **IMPORTANT** *than* **Parenting**. *This I believe.*

–Ben Carson

3 THE BASICS

"Listen to the desires of your children. Encourage them and then give them the autonomy to make their own decision."
~ *Denis Waitley*

Before discussing ways through which you can help your child with homework, it is important to discuss why teachers assign homework and how it benefits your child.

Why Do Teachers Assign Homework?

Teachers assign homework for many reasons. Homework can help their students:

- review and practice what they've covered in class;
- get ready for the next day's class;
- learn to use resources, such as libraries, reference materials and computer websites to find information about a subject;

- explore subjects more than classroom time permits;
- extend learning by applying skills they already have to new situations; and
- integrate their learning by applying many different skills to a single task, such as book reports or science projects.

Homework can also help students to develop good study habits and positive attitudes. It can:

- teach them to work independently; and
- encourage self-discipline and responsibility (assignments provide some children with their first chance to manage time and to meet deadlines).

In addition, homework can help to create greater understanding between families and teachers and provide opportunities for increased communication. Monitoring homework keeps families informed about what their children are learning and about the policies and programs of the teacher and the school.

Does Homework Help Children Learn?

Homework helps your child do better in school when the assignments are meaningful, are completed successfully and are returned to him with constructive comments from the teacher. An assignment should have a specific purpose, come with clear instructions, be fairly well matched to a child's abilities and help to develop a child's knowledge and skills.

In the *early grades,* homework can help children to develop the good study habits and positive attitudes described earlier. From *third through sixth grades,* small amounts of homework, gradually increased each year, may support improved school achievement. In *seventh grade and beyond,* students who complete more homework score better on standardized tests and earn better grades, on the average, than do students who do less homework. The difference in test scores and grades between students who do more homework and those who do less increases as students move up through the grades.

What's the Right Amount of Homework?

The right amount of homework depends on the age and skills of the child. National organizations of parents and teachers suggest that children in *kindergarten through second grade* can benefit from 10 to 20 minutes of homework each school day. In *third through sixth grades,* children can benefit from 30 to 60 minutes a school day. In *seventh through ninth grades,* students can benefit from spending more time on homework and the amount may vary from night to night.

Amounts that vary from these guidelines are fine for some children and in some situations. For example, because reading at home is especially important for children, reading assignments might push the time on homework a bit beyond the amounts suggested here.

If you are concerned that your child has either too much or too little homework, talk with his/her teacher and learn about his/her homework policies.

xxx

"Let us Sacrifice our Today so that our Children can have Better Tomorrow."

-APJ Abdul Kalam

4 HOW TO HELP: SHOW THAT YOU THINK EDUCATION AND HOMEWORK ARE IMPORTANT

"Listen to the desires of your children. Encourage them and then give them the autonomy to make their own decision."
~ *Denis Waitley*

Children need to know that their family members think homework is important. If they know their families care, children have a good reason to complete assignments and to turn them in on time. You can do many things to show that your child that you value education and homework.

First Follow Some Basic Tips

- Set aside time for homework. Make sure that your child knows that it is homework time and it is non negotiable.

- Create an environment that is favourable to doing homework. It helps if there is a permanent space where children can do homework.
- Make sure that your child knows that the TV will be turned off during homework time.
- Try to keep a bottle of water on the homework table and encourage your child to drink, to keep the brain hydrated.
- Be available to answer questions, but make sure you do not do your child's homework for them.
- If your child is working for long periods of time, stop for a hot drink or fruit break. If they are showing signs of fatigue, put some lively music on for a couple of minutes to perk them up.
- You could play classical music softly in the background or a motivational affirmation CD such as Believe and Achieve.
- If your child is studying at their computer for long periods of time, make sure they close their eyes, take a walk or breathe in some fresh air.

Now let us read a few things in detail.

Set a Regular Time for Homework

Having a regular time to do homework helps children to finish assignments. The best schedule is one that works for your child and your family. What works well in one household may not work in another. Of course, a good schedule depends in part on your child's age as well as his/her specific needs. For instance, one child may do homework best in the afternoon, completing homework first or after an hour of play and another may do it best after dinner. However, don't let your child leave homework to do just before bedtime.

Your child's outside activities, such as sports or music lessons, may mean that you need a flexible homework schedule. Your child may study after school on some days and after dinner on others. If there isn't enough time to finish homework, your child may need to drop some outside activity. Let him know that homework is a high priority.

You'll need to work with your elementary school child to develop a schedule. An older student can probably make up a schedule independently, although you'll want to make sure that it's a workable one. You may find it helpful to write out his/her schedule and put it in a place where you'll see it often, such as on the refrigerator door.

Some families have a required amount of time that their children must devote to homework or some other learning activities each school night (the length of time can vary depending upon the child's age). For instance, if your seventh grader knows he's expected to spend an hour doing homework, reading or visiting the library, he may be less likely to rush through assignments so that he can watch TV. A required amount of time may also discourage him from "forgetting" to bring home assignments and help him adjust to a routine.

Pick a Place

Your child's homework area doesn't have to be fancy. A desk in the bedroom is nice, but for many children, the kitchen table or a corner of the living room works just fine. The area should have good lighting and it should be fairly quiet.

Your child may enjoy decorating a special area for homework. A plant, a brightly colored container to hold pencils and some favorite artwork taped to the walls can make homework time more pleasant.

Remove Distractions

Turn off the TV and discourage your child from making and receiving social telephone calls during homework time. (A call to a classmate about an assignment, however, may be helpful).

Some children work well with quiet background music, but loud noise from the CD player, radio or TV is not OK. One history teacher laments, "I've actually had a kid turn in an assignment that had written in the middle, 'And Jawaharlal Nehru said, "Ohhhhh, I love you."' The kid was so plugged into the music that he wasn't concentrating."

If you live in a small or noisy household, try having all family members take part in a quiet activity during homework time. You may need to take a noisy toddler outside or into another room to play. If distractions can't be avoided, your child may want to complete assignments in the local library.

Provide Supplies and Identify Resources

Have available pencils, pens, erasers, writing paper and a dictionary. Other supplies that might be helpful include a stapler, paper clips, maps, a calculator, a pencil sharpener, tape, glue, paste, scissors, a ruler, a calculator, index cards, a thesaurus and an almanac. If possible, keep these items together in one place. If you can't provide your child with needed supplies, check with his/her teacher, school guidance counselor or principal about possible sources of assistance.

For books and other information resources, such as suitable computer websites, check with the school library or your local public library. Some libraries have homework centers designed especially to assist children with school assignments (they may even have tutors and other kinds of individual assistance).

You may want to ask your child's teacher to explain school policy about the use of computers for homework. Certainly, computers are great learning and homework tools. Your child can use his computer not only for writing reports and for getting information through

Internet resource sites, but for "talking" with teachers and classmates about assignments. In many schools, teachers post information about homework assignments and class work on their own websites, which also may have an electronic bulletin board on which students can post questions for the teacher and others to answer. However, you don't have to have a computer in your home for your child to complete homework assignments successfully. Some schools may offer after school programs that allow your child to use the school computers. And many public libraries make computers available to children.

Set a Good Example

Show your child that the skills he is learning are an important part of the things he will do as an adult. Let him see you reading books, newspapers and computer screens; writing reports, letters, e-mails and lists; using math to balance your checkbook or to measure for new carpeting; doing other things that require thought and effort. Tell your child about what you do at work.

Help your child to use everyday routines to support the skills he is learning — for example, teach him to play word and math games; help him to look up information about things in which he is interested — singers, athletes, cars, space travel and so forth; and talk with him about what he sees and hears as the two of you walk through the neighborhood, go shopping at the mall or visit a zoo or museum.

Be Interested and Interesting

Make time to take your child to the library to check out materials needed for homework (and for enjoyment) and read with your child as often as you can. Talk about school and learning activities in family conversations. Ask your child what was discussed in class that day. If he doesn't have much to say, try another approach. For example, ask him to read aloud a story he wrote or to talk about what he found out from a science experiment.

Attend school activities, such as parent-teacher meetings/conferences, plays, concerts, open houses and sports events. If you can, volunteer to help in your child's classroom or at special events. Getting to know some of your child's classmates and their parents builds a support network for you and your child. It also shows your child that his home and school are a team.

xxx

5 HOW TO HELP: MONITOR ASSIGNMENTS

"You never hear of a mother cursing the child; she is forgiving, always forgiving."
~ *Swami Vivekananda*

Children are more likely to complete homework successfully when parents monitor their assignments. How closely you need to monitor your child depends upon his age, how independent he is and how well he does in school. Whatever the age of your child, if he is not getting assignments done satisfactorily, he requires more supervision.

Here are some ways to monitor your child's assignments.

Ask about the School's Homework Policy

At the start of the school year, ask your child's teacher about any rules or guidelines that children are expected to follow as they complete homework. Ask about the kinds of assignments that will be given and the purposes for the assignments.

Most of the schools in the primary level give worksheets and assignments too. The students are given instructions to complete the homework. The children must be told to be careful at school and listen to instructions.

Talk with the teacher about your role in helping with homework. Expectations for parent involvement vary from teacher to teacher. Some teachers want parents to monitor homework closely, whereas others want them simply to check to make sure the assignment is completed on time.

Ask the teacher to call if any problems with homework come up. Let him know that you will do the same.

Be Available

Many elementary school students often like to have someone with them to answer questions as they work on assignments. If your child is cared for by someone else, talk to that caregiver about how to deal with homework. For an older child, if no one will be around, let him know when you want him to begin work and call to remind him if necessary.

However, if the teacher has made it known that students are to do homework on their own, limit your assistance to your child to assuring that assignments are clear and that necessary supplies are provided. Too much parent involvement can make children dependent — and takes away from the value of homework as a way for children to become independent and responsible.

Look over Completed Assignments

It's usually a good idea to check to see that your elementary school child has finished his/her assignments. If your middle-school student is having trouble finishing assignments, check his/her work, too. After the teacher returns completed homework, read the comments to see if your child has done the assignment satisfactorily.

Monitor Time Spent Viewing TV and Playing Video Games

In India, children on average spend far more time watching TV or playing video games than they do completing homework. In many homes, more homework gets done when TV viewing and "game" time is limited.

Once you and your child have worked out a homework schedule, take time to discuss how much TV and what programs he can watch. It's worth noting that television can be a learning tool. Look for programs that relate to what your child is studying in school, such as programs on history or science or dramatizations of children's literature. When you can, watch shows with your child, discuss them and encourage follow-up activities such as reading or a trip to the museum.

Likewise, limit the amount of time your child spends playing video games. As with TV programs, be aware of the games he likes to play and discuss his choices with him.

xxx

6 HOW TO HELP: PROVIDE GUIDANCE

"Parenting is the most important job on the planet next to keeping Gary Busey off the nation's highways."
~ *Dennis Miller*

The basic rule is, "Don't do the assignments yourself." It's not your homework – it's your child's. "I've had kids hand in homework that's in their parents' handwriting," one eighth-grade teacher complains. Doing assignments for your child won't helphim understand and use information. And it won't help him become confident in his own abilities.

Here are some ways that you can provide guidance without taking over your child's homework.

Help Your Child to Get Organized

Help your child to make a schedule and put it in a place where you'll see it often. Writing out assignments will get him used to the idea of keeping track of what's due and when. If your child is not yet able to write, write it for him until he can do it him.

A book bag or backpack will make it easier for your child to carry homework to and from school. Providing homework folders in which your child can tuck his/her assignments for safekeeping also can help him to stay organized.

Encourage Good Study Habits

Teachers generally give students tips on how to study. But it takes time and practice to develop good study habits. To reinforce good habits at home, you can:

- **Help your child manage time to complete assignments.** For example, if your eighth grader has a biology report due in three weeks, discuss all the steps he needs to take to complete it on time, including:

- selecting a topic;
- doing the research by looking up books and other materials on the topic and taking notes;
- figuring out what questions to discuss;
- drafting an outline;
- writing a rough draft; and
- revising and completing the final draft.

Encourage your child to make a chart that shows how much time he expects to spend on each step.

- **Help your child to get started when he has to do research reports or other big assignments.** Encourage him to use the library. If he isn't sure where to begin, tell him to ask the librarian for suggestions. If he's using a computer for online reference resources whether the computer is at home, school or the library make sure he's getting whatever help he needs to use it properly and to find age-appropriate Web sites. Many public libraries have homework centers with tutors or other kinds of one-on-one assistance. After your child has completed the research, listen as he tells you the points he wants to make in the report.

- **Give practice tests.** Help your third grader prepare for a spelling test by saying the words as he writes them. Have him correct his own test as you spell each word.

- **Help your child in avoiding last-minute cramming.** Review with your fifth grader how and what to study for his/her social studies test long before it's to be given. You can havehim work out a schedule of what he needs to do to, make up a practice test and write down answers to the questions he's made up.
- **Talk with your child about how to take a test.** Be sure he understands how important it is to read the instructions carefully, to keep track of

the time and to avoid spending too much time on any one question.

Talk about the Assignments

Talking and asking questions can help your child to think through an assignment and break it down into small, manageable parts. Here are some questions to ask:

- **Do you understand what you're supposed to do?** After your child has read the instructions, ask him to tell you in his own words what the assignment is about. (If he can't read yet, the teacher may have sent home instructions that you can read to him). Some schools have homework hotlines that you can call or websites that you can access by computer for assignments in case your child misplaced a paper or was absent on the day it was given. If your child doesn't understand the instructions, read them with him and talk about the assignment. Does it have words that he doesn't know? How can he find out what the words mean? If neither you nor your child understands an assignment, call one of his classmates or get in touch with the teacher.

- **Do you need help in understanding how to do this assignment?** See if your child needs to learn more, for example, about subtracting fractions before he can do his assignment. Or find out if the teacher needs to explain to him again when to use different kinds of punctuation marks. If you understand the subject yourself, you may want to work through some examples with your child. However, always lethim do the assignmenthimself.

- **Do you have everything you need to do the assignment?** Sometimes your child needs special supplies, such as colored pencils, metric rulers, calculators, maps or reference books. Check with the teacher, school guidance counselor or principal for possible sources of assistance if you can't provide the needed supplies. Check with your local library or school library for books and other information resources.

- **Does your answer make sense to you?** To check that yo ur child understands what he is doing, ask him to explain how he solved a math problem or have him summarize what he has written in a report.

Watch for Frustration

If your child shows signs of frustration, let him take a break. Encourage him and let him see that you know he can do the work.

Shower Praise

People of all ages respond to praise. And children need encouragement from the people whose opinions they value most — their families. "Good, first draft of your book report!" or "You've done a great job" can go a long way towards motivating your child to complete assignments.

Children also need to know when they haven't done their best work. Make criticism constructive, however. Instead of telling a sixth grader, "You aren't going to hand in *that* mess, are you?" say, "The teacher will understand your ideas better if you use your best handwriting." Then give praise when the child finishes a neat version.

Three Stages of Homework

- **The think-through:** Parents ask the child questions to help the child clarify what they are supposed to do. This is to bring back their short-term memory of what they have been taught. How long should this essay be? What do you always need to put at the end of a sentence? How will you show the teacher how you did this sum? Based on what the parent knows of their child's habits you will know what questions to ask.

- **The Doing:** It will be much quicker. The child focuses more. The child knows what they are supposed to do and how. During stage 2 the parents give no help whatsoever. If your child needs any help, you refer back to stage 1. It's about doing it on his own. It is intended to be done by the pupil, it is not intended to be a collaborative effort.

- **Improvement stage:** The day after the child has done the homework, the pupil says two things that are good about the work, and the parent says two things that are good. In addition to this the pupil and parent each have to mention two things that need to improve. For example, make your small letter small, your tall letter tall. This irons out a lot of things that need to happen, there will be far fewer mistakes, which is always very wonderful.

xxx

7 HOW TO HELP: TALK WITH TEACHERS TO RESOLVE PROBLEMS

"Parenting makes us better in so many regards."
~ *Alissa Quart*

Homework problems often can be avoided when families and caregivers value, monitor and guide their children's work on assignments. Sometimes, however, helping in these ways is not enough. If you have problems, here are some suggestions for how to deal with them.

Tell the Teacher about Your Concerns

You may want to contact the teacher if:

- your child refuses to do his assignments, even though you've tried hard to get him to do them;
- the instructions are unclear;
- you can't seem to help your child get organized to finish the assignments;
- you can't provide needed supplies or materials;
- neither you nor your child can understand the purpose of the assignments;
- the assignments are too hard or too easy;
- the homework is assigned in uneven amounts – for instance, no homework is given on Monday, Tuesday or Wednesday, but on Thursday four assignments are made that are due the next day; or
- your child has missed school and needs to make up assignments.

In some cases, the school guidance counselor or principal also may be helpful in resolving problems.

Work with the Teacher

Continuing communication with teachers is very important in solving homework problems. As you work with your child's teacher, here are some important things to remember:

- **Talk with each of your child's teachers early in the school year.** Get acquainted *before* problems arise and let each teacher know that you want to be kept informed. Most elementary and middle schools hold regular parent-teacher conferences or open houses. If your child's school doesn't provide such opportunities, call the teacher to set up a meeting.

- **Contact the teacher as soon as you suspect your child has a homework problem** (as well as when you think he's having any major problems with his schoolwork). Schools have a responsibility to keep you informed about your child's performance and behavior and you have a right to be upset if you don't find out until report-card time that your child is having difficulties. On the other hand, you may figure out that a problem exists before the teacher does. By alerting the teacher, you can work together to solve a problem in its early stages.
- **Request a meeting with the teacher to discuss homework problems.** Tell him briefly why you want to meet. You might say, "Rachel is having trouble with her math homework. I'm

worried about why she can't finish the problems and what we might do to help her." If English is your second language, you may need to make special arrangements, such as including in the meeting someone who is bilingual.

Approach the teacher with a cooperative spirit. Believe that the teacher wants to help you and your child, even if you disagree about something. Don't go to the principal without giving the teacher a chance to work out the problem with you and your child.

- **Let the teacher know whether your child finds the assignments too hard or too easy.** (Teachers also like to know when their students are particularly excited about an assignment.) Of course, not all homework assignments can be expected to interest your child and be perfectly suited to him. Teachers just don't have time to tailor homework to the individual needs of each student. However, most teachers want to assign homework that their students can complete successfully and they welcome feedback.

Many teachers structure homework so that a wide range of students will find assignments interesting. For example:

- They offer students options for different approaches to the same topic or lesson;
- They give extra assignments to students who want more challenge; and
- They give specialized assignments to students who are having trouble in a particular area.

• **During your meeting with the teacher, explain what you think is going on.** In addition, tell the teacher if you don't know what the problem is. Sometimes a student's version of what's going on isn't the same as the teacher's version. For example, your child may tell you that the teacher never explains assignments so that he can understand them. But the teacher may tell you that your child isn't paying attention when assignments are given.

• **Work out a way to solve or lessen the problem.** The strategy will depend on what the problem is, how severe it is and what the needs of your child are. For instance:

- Is the homework often too hard? Maybe your child has fallen behind and will need extra help from the teacher or a tutor to catch up.
- Does your child need to make up a lot of work because of absences? The first step might be working out a schedule with the teacher.
- Does your child need extra support beyond what home and school can give her? Ask the teacher, school guidance counselor or principal if there are mentor programs in your community. Mentor programs pair a child with an adult volunteer who assists with the child's special needs. Many schools, universities, community organizations, churches and businesses offer excellent mentoring programs.

- **Make sure that communication is clear.** Listen to the teacher and don't leave until you're sure that you understand what's being said. Make sure too, that the teacher understands what you have to say. If, after the meeting, you realize you don't understand something, call the teacher to clarify.

At the end of the meeting, it may help to summarize what you've agreed to do:

OK, so to keep track of Kim's assignments, I'll check her assignment book each night and write my initials beside new assignments. Each day you'll check to make sure she's written down all new assignments in her book. That way we'll be certain that I know what her assignments are.

- **Follow up to make sure that the approach you agreed to is working.** If the teacher told you, for example, that your child needs to spend more time practising long division, check back in a month to talk about your child's progress.

Homework can bring together children, families and teachers in a common effort to improve children's learning.

Helping your child with homework is an opportunity to improve your child's chances of doing well in school and life. By helping your child with homework, you can help him learn important lessons about discipline and responsibility. You can open up lines of communication — between you and your child and you and the school. You are in a unique position to help your child make connections between school work and the "real world," and thereby bring meaning (and some enjoyment) to your child's homework experience.

×××

"Love your children more than your ego.
Love your children enough to allow them to progress through childhood as non-perfect beings, who are a work in progress, just like you are."
-Nicholeen Peck

HOMEWORK TIPS FOR PARENTS

"Always kiss your children goodnight, even if they're already asleep."
~ *H. Jackson Brown, Jr.*

General Homework Tips

- **Make sure your child has a quiet, well-lit place to do homework.** Avoid having your child do homework with the mobile, television on or in places with other distractions, such as people coming and going.
- **Make sure the materials your child needs, such as paper, pencils and a dictionary, are available.** Ask your child if special materials will be needed for some projects and get them in advance.

- **Help your child with time management.** Establish a set time each day for doing homework. Don't let your child leave homework until just before bedtime. Think about using a weekend morning or afternoon for working on big projects, especially if the project involves getting together with classmates.
- **Be positive about homework.** Tell your child how important school is. The attitude you express about homework will be the attitude your child acquires.
- **When your child does homework, you do homework.** Show your child that the skills they are learning are related to things you do as an adult. If your child is reading, you read too. If your child is doing math, balance your checkbook.
- **When your child asks for help, provide guidance, not answers.** Giving answers means your child will not learn the material. Too much help teaches your child that when the going gets rough, someone will do the work for him.
- **When the teacher asks that you play a role in homework, do it.** Cooperate with the teacher. It shows your child that the school and home are a team. Follow the directions given by the teacher.
- **If homework is meant to be done by your child alone, stay away.** Too much parental involvement can prevent homework from having

some positive effects. Homework is a great way for kids to develop independent, life long learning skills.

- **Stay informed.** Talk with your child's teacher. Make sure you know the purpose of homework and what your child's class rules are.
- **Help your child figure out what is hard homework and what is easy homework.** Have your child do the hard work first. This will mean he will be most alert when facing the biggest challenges. Easy material will seem to go fast when fatigue begins to set in.
- **Watch your child for signs of failure and frustration.** Let your child take a short break if he is having trouble keeping his mind on an assignment.
- **Reward progress in homework.** If your child has been successful in homework completion and is working hard, celebrate that success with a special event (e.g., zoo, planetarium, disney land, a trip to the park) to reinforce the positive effort.

Reading Homework Tips

- Have your child read aloud to you every night.
- Choose a quiet place, free from distractions, for your child to do his nightly reading assignments.
- As your child reads, point out spelling and sound patterns such as *cat, pat, hat.*

- When your child reads aloud to you and makes a mistake, point out the words he has missed and help him to read the word correctly.
- After your child has stopped to correct a word he has read, have him go back and reread the entire sentence from the beginning to make sure he understands what the sentence is saying.

- Ask your child to tell you in his own words what happened in a story.
- To check your child's understanding of what he is reading, occasionally pause and ask your child questions about the characters and events in the story.
- Ask your child why he thinks a character acted in a certain way and tell him to support his answer with information from the story.
- Before getting to the end of a story, ask your child what he thinks will happen next and why.

Math Homework Tips

- Encourage your child to use a daily math assignment book.
- Follow the progress your child is making in math. Check with your child daily about his homework.
- If you don't understand your child's math assignments, engage in frequent communication with his teacher.
- If your child is experiencing problems in math, contact the teacher to learn whether he is working at grade level and what can be done at home to help improve academic progress.
- Request that your child's teacher schedule after-school math tutoring sessions if your child really needs help.
- Advocate with the principal for the use of research-based peer tutoring programs for math. These tutoring programs have proven results, and students really enjoy them.
- Use household chores as opportunities for reinforcing math learning such as cooking and repair activities.
- Try to be aware of how your child is being taught math, and don't teach strategies and shortcuts that conflict with the approach the teacher is using. Check in with the teacher and ask what you can do to help. Ask the teacher about online resources that you can use for your child at home.

- At the beginning of the year, ask your child's teacher for a list of suggestions that will enable you to help your child with math homework.

×××

The best security blanket a child can have is parents who respect each others.

-Jane Blaustone

CHECKLIST FOR HELPING YOUR CHILD WITH HOMEWORK

"Parenthood remains the greatest single preserve of the amateur."
~ *Alvin Toffler*

1. Show that You Think Education and Homework are Important

- Do you set a regular time every day for homework?
- Does your child have the papers, books, pencils and other things needed to do assignments?
- Does your child have a well-lit, fairly quiet place to study?
- Do you set a good example by showing your child that the skills he is learning are an important part of the things he will do as an adult?
- Do you stay in touch with your child's teacher?

2. Monitor Assignments

- Do you know what your child's homework assignments are? How long they should take? How the teacher wants you to be involved in them?
- Do you see that your child starts and completes assignments?
- Do you read the teacher's comments on assignments that are returned?
- Is TV viewing or video game playing cutting into your child's homework time?

3. Provide Guidance

- Do you help your child to get organized? Does your child need a schedule or assignment book? A book bag or backpack and a folder for papers?
- Do you encourage your child to develop good study habits (for example, scheduling enough time for big assignments; making up practice tests)?
- Do you talk with your child about homework assignments? Does he understand them?

4. Talk with Teachers to Resolve Problems

- Do you meet with the teacher early in the year *before* any problems arise?
- If a problem comes up, do you meet with the teacher?

- Do you cooperate with the teacher to work out a plan and a schedule to solve homework problems?
- Do you follow up with the teacher and with your child to make sure the plan is working?

♦♦♦

RESOURCES

"Listen to the desires of your children. Encourage them and then give them the autonomy to make their own decision."
~ *Denis Waitley*

The following publications provide more information about how to help your child with homework.

- Homework without Tears: A Parent's Guide for Motivating Children to Do Homework and to Succeed in School, Canter, Lee and Hausner, Lee. (1993). New York: HarperCollins.
- The Homework Handbook: Practical Advice You Can Use Tonight to Help Your Child Succeed Tomorrow: Cholden, Harriet, Friedman, John A. and Tiersky, Ethel. (1998). New York: McGraw-Hill.

- The Battle over Homework: Common Ground for Administrators, Teachers and Parents: Cooper, Harris M. (2001). New York: Corwin Press.
- Taming the Homework Monster: How to Stop Fighting with Your Kids over Homework: Klavan, Ellen. (1992). New York: Poseidon Press.

Understand Your Child: Teen and Child Personality Test

http://www.personalitylab.org/tests/bfi2_parent_outs.htm

National Sources of Assistance If Your Child Has a Learning Disability

- **The Association of Learning Disabilities of India**

  Reg No. (297/95)

  ALDI Learning Centre

  Nellankara, Nettissery P.O.

  Thrissur - 680657, India

  Tel: + 91 487 2336817

  email: joseph.aldindia@gmail.com

- **Karmayog**

  C/o Shri R. O. Somani Charitable Trust

  Shreeniwas House, 2nd floor

  (Behind Bombay Gymkhana)

  H. Somani Road, Fort

  Mumbai 400001

- **Orkids**

  E-123, Kalkaji

  New Delhi – 110019

  Ph: 011- 40529564, 26439535

  http://www.orkidsped.com

- **Shristi Learning Centre**

  Dr. Rajiv Nandy

  C-272, Vivek Vihar, Near Vivekanand Mahilla College

  New Delhi, Delhi - 110 053, India

  E-mail : shristilearn@gmail.com

  Mobile: +(91)-9810021054

- **Bharatiya Vidya Bhavan**

  Kasturba Gandhi Marg, New Delhi-110001; Phone: 23389943, 23384881

  Focus Area: Slow Learner.

- **Child Guidance Center**

  National Institute of Public Cooperation & Child Development,

  5, Siri Institutional Area, Hauz Khas, New Delhi-110016; Phone: 2696 3002/3204/3378

  Focus Area: Multiple disability; Speech problem; Slow learners in the age groups 0-14; Scholastic problems.

- **Child Guidance Center**

  Zakir Hussain Memorial Welfare Society,

  Jamia Millia Islamia (T T T), New Delhi-110025;

  Phone: 26842554(R), 26843909

  Focus Area: Mentally ill; Behavioural and speech problems; Educational problems.

- **Child Guidance Clinic**

  Department of Psychiatry AIIMS,

  New Delhi-110029;

  Phone: 26594412

  Focus Area: Mentally ill; Slow learners; Psychological disorders.

- **Jan Madhyam**

  148 Zamrudpur, New Delhi-110048;

  Phone: 26473525 Fax: 26473525

  e-mail: jmadhayam@yahoo.com

  Focus Area: Multiple disability; learning disabilities; Intellectual disabilities.

- **Sadhu Vaswani International School Girls**

  2nd Street, Shanti Niketan, New Delhi;

  Phone: 24670242, 26872390

  Focus Area: Slow learner.

- **St. Thomas Girls Senior Secondary**

  Mandir Marg, New Delhi-110001;

  Phone: 23364094

  Focus Area: Slow learner

xxx

History will judge us by the difference we make in the everyday lives of children.

-Nelson Mandela

The Books that will give you Knowledge, Awareness and Remove your Misconceptions

DON'T ONLY DREAM, MAKE IT TRUE.

We give wings to your

DREAMS

PUBLISH BOOK AND BECOME AN AUTHOR

We will help you to write and share it with world

Visit: Gullybaba.com